W9-AXZ-138

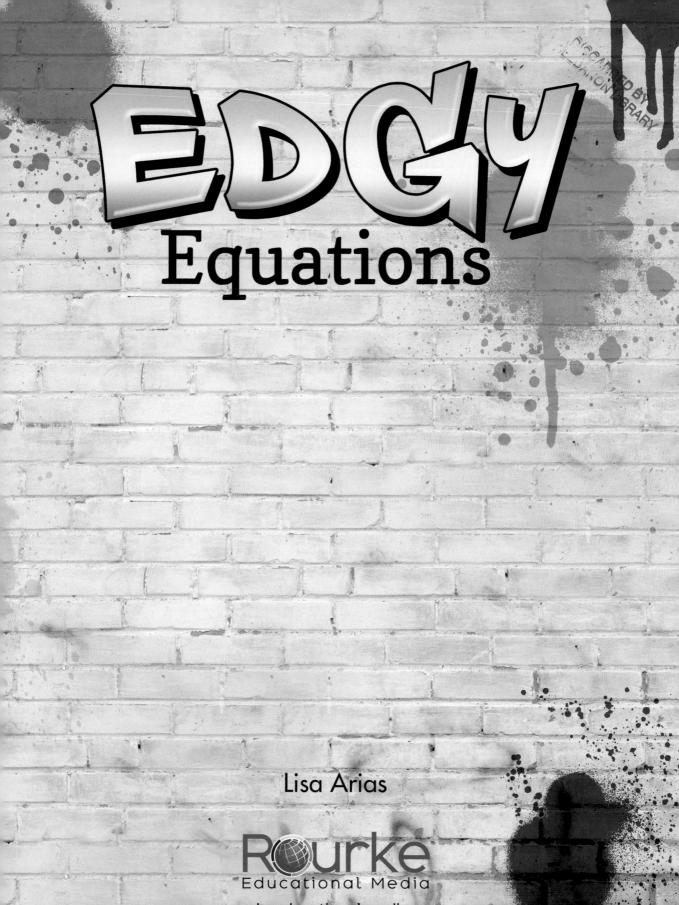

EDGY
Equations

Lisa Arias

Rourke
Educational Media

rourkeeducationalmedia.com

Scan for Related Titles
and Teacher Resources

Before Reading:

Building Academic Vocabulary and Background Knowledge

Before reading a book, it is important to tap into what your child or students already know about the topic. This will help them develop their vocabulary, increase their reading comprehension, and make connections across the curriculum.

1. Look at the cover of the book. What will this book be about?
2. What do you already know about the topic?
3. Let's study the Table of Contents. What will you learn about in the book's chapters?
4. What would you like to learn about this topic? Do you think you might learn about it from this book? Why or why not?
5. Use a reading journal to write about your knowledge of this topic. Record what you already know about the topic and what you hope to learn about the topic.
6. Read the book.
7. In your reading journal, record what you learned about the topic and your response to the book.
8. After reading the book complete the activities below.

Content Area Vocabulary
Read the list. What do these words mean?

algebra
bar diagrams
denominator
dividend
division bar
divisor
equations
inverse operations
operations
reciprocation
variable

After Reading:

Comprehension and Extension Activity

After reading the book, work on the following questions with your child or students in order to check their level of reading comprehension and content mastery.

1. Explain the importance of understanding inverse operations. (Summarize)
2. What is the purpose of the variable in equations? (Asking questions)
3. Have you ever needed to solve for an unknown amount while at the store? Explain. (Text to self connection)
4. Can you always be correct when you solve for a variable? Explain. (Asking questions)
5. Why does multiplication look different in algebra compared to math? (Summarize)

Extension Activity

Now it's time for you to be the teacher! Grab a parent or friend and teach them about inverse operations and how to solve for the variable. Did you use the book to help you teach the concept? Did you have to use pictures and examples to help your parent or friend understand? What are some strategies you used that helped them learn about inverse operations and solving for the variable?

TABLE OF CONTENTS

EQUATIONS YOU SAY?

Today is the day for equations to head our way.

Equations are math sentences with equal signs.

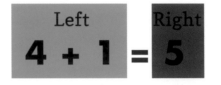

Left	Right
4 + 1 =	5

Left	Right
13 =	13

Left	Right
10 – 2 =	8

Left	Right
3 × 2 =	6

The equal sign separates an equation into two equal parts.

For an equation to be true, the value to the left must be equal to the value on the right.

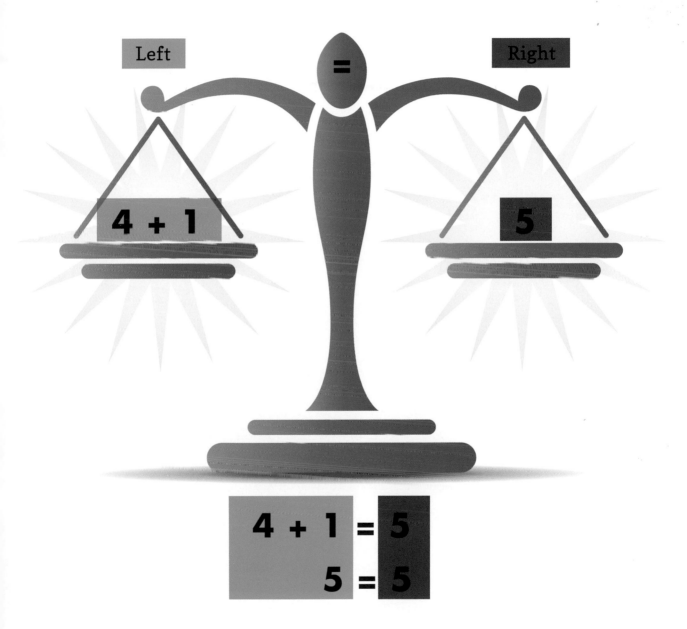

You will soon see that balance is key!

MATH VERSUS ALGEBRA

Using math facts is the thing to do
when the numbers and **operations** are given to you.

The mystery has been solved!
Math becomes **algebra** when **variables** are involved.

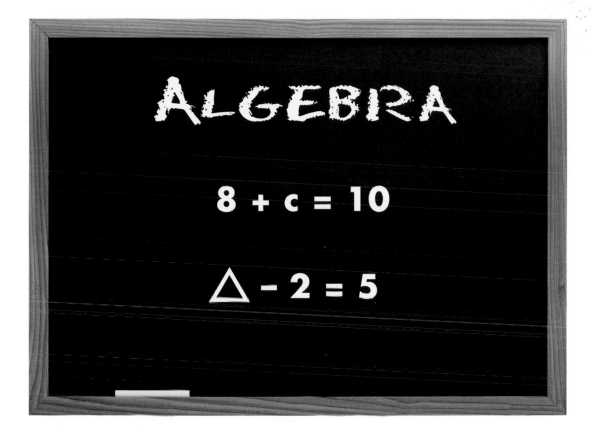

ALGEBRA

$$8 + c = 10$$

$$\triangle - 2 = 5$$

Check It Out!

Variables are letters or symbols in place of unknown numbers. When using a letter as a variable, it should always be written as a lower case letter.

Incorrect	Correct
$3 + Z = 9$	$3 + z = 9$

$$7 \times z = 14$$

In algebra, the multiplication sign is banned. It looks too much like a variable. Here are some ways that multiplication is shown in algebra.

	Parenthesis	Dot	Touching
Seven times z	**7(z)**	**7 • z**	**7z** (only with a variable and **coefficient**)
Four times eight	**4(8)**	**4 • 8**	

A coefficient is the number in front of the variable.

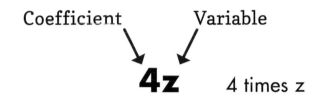

4z   4 times z

If a variable stands alone, the coefficient is 1.

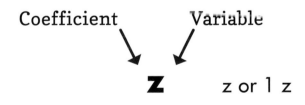

z   z or 1 z

INVERSE OPERATIONS

Addition and Subtraction

Addition and subtraction are **inverse operations**.

Use subtraction to undo addition. The inverse of +3 is -3.

If there are 3 birds in a tree and they fly away,
there are none, so now the inverse is done!

+ 3   − 3   = 0

Use addition to undo subtraction. The inverse of -5 is +5.

If you take five scoops of dirt and then put five scoops back, the inverse is done because the hole is gone!

– 5   **+ 5**   **= 0**

Multiplication and Division

Multiplication and division are inverse operations.
Use division to undo multiplication. The inverse of multiplying by 3 is to divide by 3.

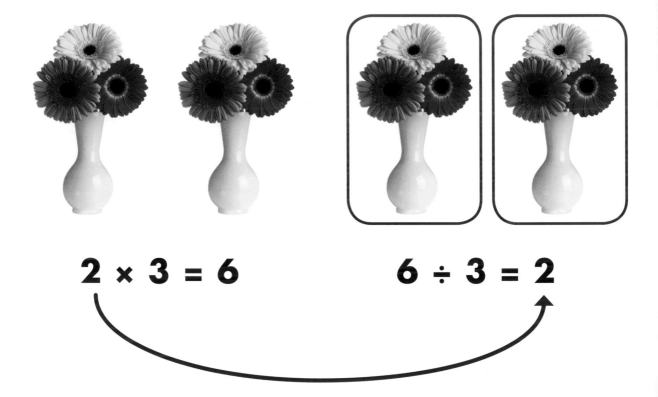

$$2 \times 3 = 6 \qquad 6 \div 3 = 2$$

Dividing by 3 was the right plan
because you are right back where you began.

Use multiplication to undo division. The inverse of dividing by 5 is to multiply by 5.

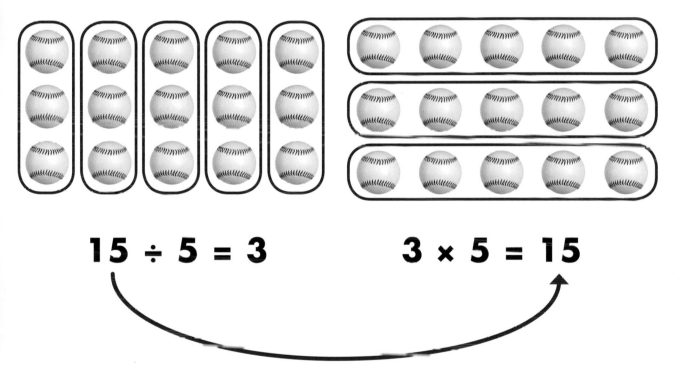

$$15 \div 5 = 3 \qquad 3 \times 5 = 15$$

Multiplying by 5 was the right plan because you are right back where you began!

Solve Equations

Now it is time for your mission,
to solve equations using inverse operations.

$$x + 2 = 15$$

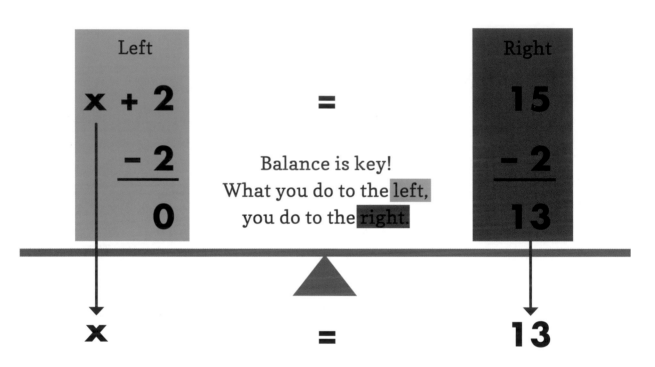

Left		Right
x + 2	=	15
- 2		- 2
0		13

Balance is key!
What you do to the left,
you do to the right.

x = 13

Use the inverse to reverse each operation, one by one,
until everything except the variable has been undone.

In the end, all that will stand is the variable and its solution.

Find the Operation to Reverse

To isolate the variable, which operation needs the inverse?

$$d - 20 = 35$$

$$\frac{a}{5} = 15$$

$$6 = k + 4$$

$$8 = 2y$$

Check It Out!

What a surprise.
Fractions are division problems in disguise!

In algebra, the division sign is just a bar.
a ÷ 5 is written just like a fraction $\frac{a}{5}$.

CHECK SOLUTIONS

Checking your solution is the key
to knowing that your work was done correctly.

$$x + 2 = 15$$

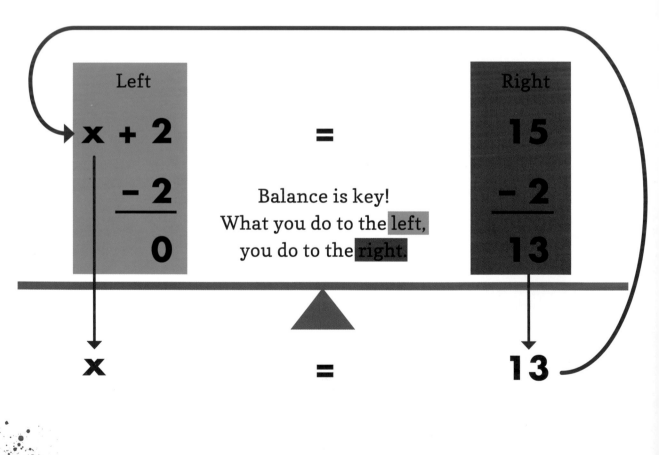

Left

$$x + 2$$

$$\begin{array}{r} -2 \\ \hline 0 \end{array}$$

=

Balance is key!
What you do to the left,
you do to the right.

Right

15

$$\begin{array}{r} -2 \\ \hline 13 \end{array}$$

$$x \qquad = \qquad 13$$

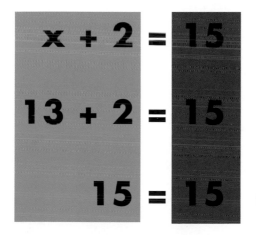

$x + 2 = 15$ Rewrite the original equation.

$13 + 2 = 15$ Replace the variable with your solution.

$15 = 15$ Solve.

As long as both sides agree, your work is right, you see!

SOLVE ADDITION EQUATIONS

Subtraction is the perfect operation to undo addition.

While at work, always recite,
"What you do to the left, you do to the right."

$$17 + y = 23$$

Check

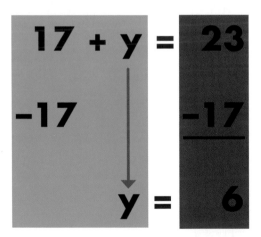

17 + y =	23
17 + 6 =	23
23 =	23 ✓

Addition Equations with Fractions

Follow the rules for fractions when they are part of the action.

$$\frac{3}{5} = \frac{1}{5} + p$$

$$\frac{3}{5} = \frac{1}{5} + p$$
$$-\frac{1}{5} \qquad -\frac{1}{5}$$
$$\frac{2}{5} = \qquad\qquad p$$

Check

$$\frac{3}{5} = \frac{1}{5} + p$$
$$\frac{3}{5} = \frac{1}{5} + \frac{2}{5}$$
$$\frac{3}{5} = \frac{3}{5} \qquad \checkmark$$

Check It Out!

Aim for the same **denominator**! Find common denominators before adding or subtracting fractions.

19

SOLVE SUBTRACTION EQUATIONS

No matter the case,
addition will always put subtraction in its place.

The same applies here and you must recite,
"What you do to the left, you do to the right."

$$f - 8 = 17$$

Check

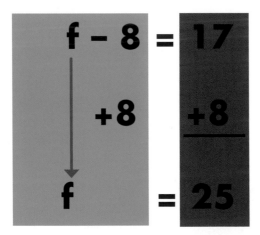

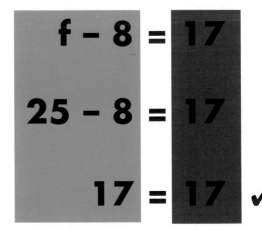

Subtraction Equations with Decimals

When decimals appear, everything is okay
as long as you obey their rules of play.

$$s - .25 = .32$$

Check

$$
\begin{array}{rl}
s - .25 &= .32 \\
+.25 & +.25 \\
\hline
s &= .57
\end{array}
$$

$$
\begin{array}{rl}
s - .25 &= .32 \\
.57 - .25 &= .32 \\
.32 &= .32 \checkmark
\end{array}
$$

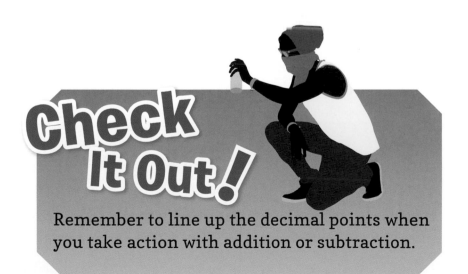

Check It Out!

Remember to line up the decimal points when
you take action with addition or subtraction.

SOLVE MULTIPLICATION EQUATIONS

The time has arrived for the **division bar** to run the show and undo multiplication like a superhero.

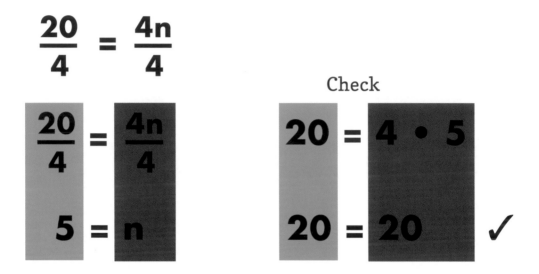

$$\frac{20}{4} = \frac{4n}{4}$$

$$\frac{20}{4} = \frac{4n}{4}$$

$$5 = n$$

Check

$$20 = 4 \cdot 5$$

$$20 = 20 \quad \checkmark$$

As we always say, "What you do to the left, you do to the right."

Multiplication Equations with Decimals

When decimals appear, everything is okay
as long as you obey their rules of play.

Never divide by a decimal. Instead, move the decimal point to the right in the **divisor** as many spaces as needed to make it a whole number. Next, move the decimal place to the right in the **dividend** the same number of places.

Time to find out how many quarters are in one dollar.

4. *New Position*

.25 ⟌ 1.00

Move the decimal two spaces to the right.

$$\frac{.50c}{.50} = \frac{2.50}{.50}$$

Check

$$\frac{.50c}{.50} = \frac{2.50}{.50}$$

$$c = 5$$

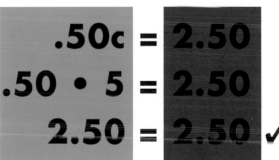

.50c = 2.50

.50 • 5 = 2.50

2.50 = 2.50 ✓

5. *New Position*

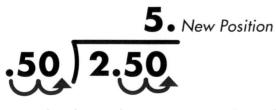

.50 ⟌ 2.50

Move the decimal two spaces to the right.

.50
× 5
‾‾‾‾
2.50

Count the decimals in each factor.

The product will have the same number of decimal places that were counted in the factors.

23

Multiply by the Reciprocal

Fractions are the trickiest multiplication combination to undo because dividing by a fraction is something you can never do.

When your mission is fraction division,
follow the rules and replace division
with multiplication and **reciprocation**.

Let's see how many halves are in four.

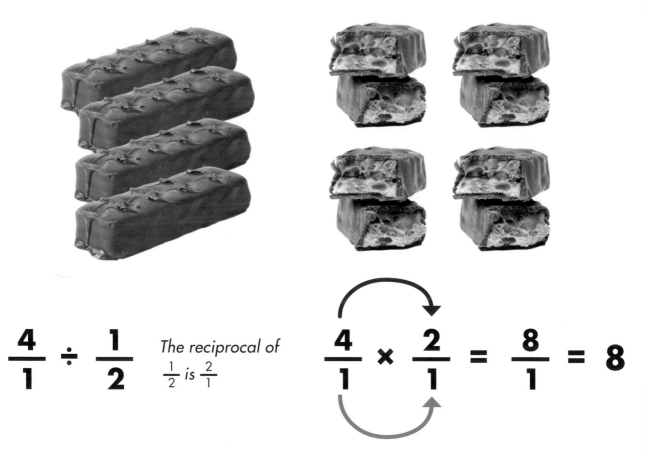

$$\frac{4}{1} \div \frac{1}{2}$$

The reciprocal of $\frac{1}{2}$ is $\frac{2}{1}$

$$\frac{4}{1} \times \frac{2}{1} = \frac{8}{1} = 8$$

Dividing by a fraction is not an allowable action.

Instead, multiply by the reciprocal.

Multiplication Equations with Fractions

$$\frac{1}{3}k = 6$$

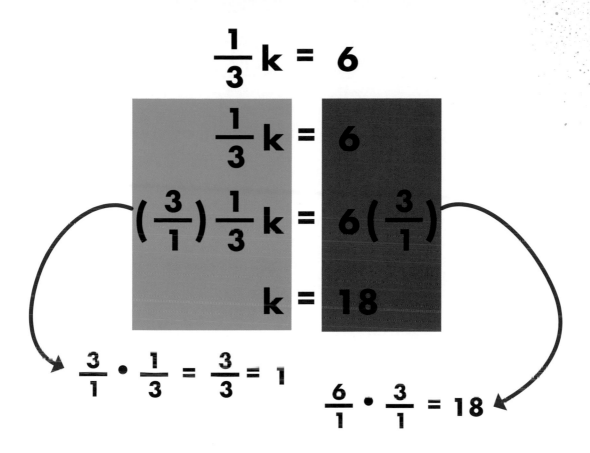

$$\frac{1}{3}k = 6$$

$$\left(\frac{3}{1}\right)\frac{1}{3}k = 6\left(\frac{3}{1}\right)$$

$$k = 18$$

$$\frac{3}{1} \cdot \frac{1}{3} = \frac{3}{3} = 1$$

$$\frac{6}{1} \cdot \frac{3}{1} = 18$$

$$\frac{1}{\cancel{3}_1} \cdot \frac{\cancel{18}^{6}}{1} = 6$$

Simplify before you multiply.

Check

$$\frac{1}{3}k = 6$$

$$\frac{1}{3} \cdot 18 = 6$$

$$6 = 6 \checkmark$$

SOLVE DIVISION EQUATIONS

Multiplication is ready to steal the show from those daring division bar stars.

With just a little fun, the division will soon be undone.

Say it again without thinking twice,
"What you do to the left, you do to the right."

$$\frac{m}{2} = 7$$

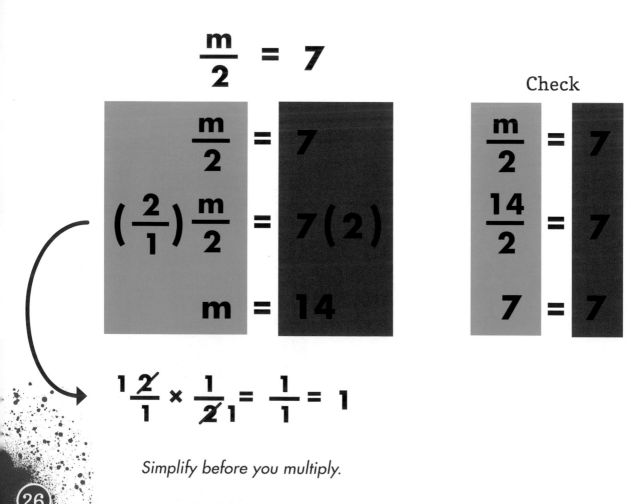

Check

$$\frac{m}{2} = 7$$

$$\left(\frac{2}{1}\right)\frac{m}{2} = 7(2)$$

$$m = 14$$

$$\frac{m}{2} = 7$$

$$\frac{14}{2} = 7$$

$$7 = 7 \checkmark$$

$$^1\frac{\cancel{2}}{1} \times \frac{1}{\cancel{2}_1} = \frac{1}{1} = 1$$

Simplify before you multiply.

Solve Division Equations with Decimals

So now you see there is no trick.
Stick to rules and those division bar stars will be gone lickety-split.

$$(1.5)\frac{f}{1.5} = 2(1.5)$$

$$(1.5)\frac{f}{1.5} = 2(1.5)$$

$$f = 3$$

Check

$$\frac{3}{1.5} = 2$$

$$2 = 2 \quad \checkmark$$

$$
\begin{array}{r}
1.5 \\
\times\ 2 \\
\hline
3.0
\end{array}
$$

$$1.5\overline{)\,30\,}\quad 2.$$

Count the decimals in each factor.

*The product will have the same
number of decimal places that
were counted in the factors.*

BAR DIAGRAMS

Bar diagrams are used to model most every situation equations can be placed in.

If a word problem ever gives you doubt, then it is time to get a bar diagram out.

The value added to the left bar must be equal to the value of the right bar.

The right bar represents the total.

Let's give bar diagrams a try.

Mrs. Lopez has $60 to spend on school supplies for her class. She has already spent $15. How much money does she have left to spend?

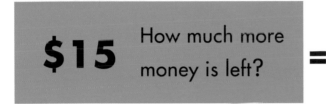

Write $15 in the left bar because it is part of the total.

The sum of $15 and the unknown amount must be equal to the total.

Write $60 in the right bar because it is the total.

15 + m = 60

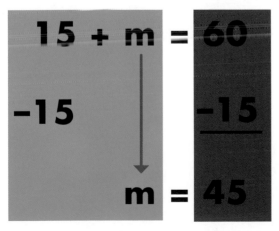

Mrs. Lopez has $45 left!

Check

GLOSSARY

algebra (AL-juh-bruh): a type of math that uses symbols or letters in place of numbers

bar diagrams (BAR DYE-uh-grams): models used to represent equations in word problems

denominator (di-NOM-uh-nay-tor): the bottom number of a fraction that shows the number of equal parts of the whole

dividend (DIV-i-dend): the number being divided up in a division problem

division bar (di-VIZH-uhn BAR): a symbol used to show division

divisor (di-VYE-zur): the number that you divide by in a division problem.

equations (i-KWAY-shuhns): a math statement showing that two expressions are equal

inverse operations (in-VURSS op-uh-RAY-shuhns): a math operation that reverses the result of another math operation

operations (op-uh-RAY-shuhnz): a mathematical action that changes a number

reciprocation (ri-SIP-ruh-kay-shuhn): to turn a fraction upside down by switching the numerator and denominator

variable (VAIR-ee-uh-buhl): a symbol or letter that represents an unknown number

INDEX

WEBSITES TO VISIT

www.math-play.com/soccer-math-one-step-equations-game/one-step-
     equations-game.html

www.funbrain.com/guess2/index.html

www.xpmath.com/forums/arcade.php?do=play&gameid=105

ABOUT THE AUTHOR

Lisa Arias is a math teacher who lives in Tampa, Florida with her husband and two children. Her out-of-the-box thinking and love for math guided her toward becoming an author. She enjoys playing board games and spending time with family and friends.

Meet The Author!
www.meetREMauthors.com

PHOTO CREDITS: Cover © Capsule; Title Page © Capsule; Page 5 © mstay; Page 6 © kate_sept2004, James G Brey; Page 7 © 4x6; Page 10 © lattesmile; Page 11 © Milos Dizajn; Page 12 © Gita Kulinitch Studios; Page 13 © GeoffBlack; Page 23 © maogg; Page 24 © TZfoto, Serts

Edited by: Jill Sherman

Cover and Interior design by: Tara Raymo

Library of Congress PCN Data

Edgy Equations: One-Variable Equations / Lisa Arias
(Got Math!)
ISBN 978-1-62717-721-4 (hard cover)
ISBN 978-1-62717-843-3 (soft cover)
ISBN 978-1-62717-956-0 (e-Book)
Library of Congress Control Number: 2014935601

Printed in the United States of America, North Mankato, Minnesota

Also Available as: